DRUG AND ALCOHOL DEPENDENCE

MENTAL ILLNESSES AND DISORDERS

Alzheimer's Disease

Anxiety Disorders

Attention-Deficit Hyperactivity Disorder

Autism Spectrum Disorders

Bipolar Disorder

Depression

Disruptive Behavior Disorders

Drug and Alcohol Dependence

Eating Disorders

Obsessive-Compulsive Disorder

Post-Traumatic Stress Disorder

Schizophrenia

Sleep Disorders

DRUG AND ALCOHOL DEPENDENCE

H.W. Poole

SERIES CONSULTANT
ANNE S. WALTERS, PhD

Chief Psychologist, Emma Pendleton Bradley Hospital

Clinical Associate Professor, Alpert Medical School/Brown University

MASON CREST

Mason Crest
450 Parkway Drive, Suite D
Broomall, PA 19008
www.masoncrest.com

MTM Publishing, Inc.
435 West 23rd Street, #8C
New York, NY 10011
www.mtmpublishing.com

President: Valerie Tomaselli
Vice President, Book Development: Hilary Poole
Designer: Annemarie Redmond
Copyeditor: Peter Jaskowiak
Editorial Assistant: Andrea St. Aubin

Series ISBN: 978-1-4222-3364-1
ISBN: 978-1-4222-3371-9
Ebook ISBN: 978-1-4222-8572-5

Library of Congress Cataloging-in-Publication Data
Poole, Hilary W., author.
  Drug and alcohol dependence / by H.W. Poole.
     pages cm. — (Mental illnesses and disorders : awareness and understanding)
  Includes bibliographical references and index.
  ISBN 978-1-4222-3371-9 (hardback) — ISBN 978-1-4222-3364-1 (series) — ISBN
978-1-4222-8572-5 (ebook)
  1. Drug addiction—Juvenile literature. 2. Alcoholism—Juvenile literature. I. Title.
  RC564.3.P66 2016
  616.86—dc23
                                                                        2015006703

Printed and bound in the United States of America.

First printing
9 8 7 6 5 4 3 2 1

TABLE OF CONTENTS

Key Icons to Look for:

Words to Understand: These words with their easy-to-understand definitions will increase the reader's understanding of the text, while building vocabulary skills.

Sidebars: This boxed material within the main text allows readers to build knowledge, gain insights, explore possibilities, and broaden their perspectives by weaving together additional information to provide realistic and holistic perspectives.

Research Projects: Readers are pointed toward areas of further inquiry connected to each chapter. Suggestions are provided for projects that encourage deeper research and analysis.

Text-Dependent Questions: These questions send the reader back to the text for more careful attention to the evidence presented there.

Series Glossary of Key Terms: This back-of-the-book glossary contains terminology used throughout the series. Words found here increase the reader's ability to read and comprehend higher-level books and articles in this field.

People who cope with mental illnesses and disorders deserve our empathy and respect.

(istockphoto/digitalskillet)

Introduction to the Series

According to the National Institute of Mental Health, in 2012 there were an estimated 45 million people in the United States suffering from mental illness, or 19 percent of all US adults. A separate 2011 study found that among children, almost one in five suffer from some form of mental illness or disorder. The nature and level of impairment varies widely. For example, children and adults with anxiety disorders may struggle with a range of symptoms, from a constant state of worry about both real and imagined events to a complete inability to leave the house. Children or adults with schizophrenia might experience periods when the illness is well controlled by medication and therapies, but there may also be times when they must spend time in a hospital for their own safety and the safety of others. For every person with mental illness who makes the news, there are many more who do not, and these are the people that we must learn more about and help to feel accepted, and even welcomed, in this world of diversity.

It is not easy to have a mental illness in this country. Access to mental health services remains a significant issue. Many states and some private insurers have "opted out" of providing sufficient coverage for mental health treatment. This translates to limits on the amount of sessions or frequency of treatment, inadequate rates for providers, and other problems that make it difficult for people to get the care they need.

Meanwhile, stigma about mental illness remains widespread. There are still whispers about "bad parenting," or "the other side of the tracks." The whisperers imply that mental illness is something you bring upon yourself, or something that someone does to you. Obviously, mental illness can be exacerbated by an adverse event such as trauma or parental instability. But there is just as much truth to the biological bases of mental illness. No one is made schizophrenic by ineffective parenting, for example, or by engaging in "wild" behavior as an adolescent. Mental illness is a complex interplay of genes, biology, and the environment, much like many physical illnesses.

People with mental illness are brave soldiers, really. They fight their illness every day, in all of the settings of their lives. When people with an anxiety disorder graduate from college, you know that they worked very hard to get there—harder, perhaps, than those who did not struggle with a psychiatric issue. They got up every day with a pit in their stomach about facing the world, and they worried about their finals more than their classmates. When they had to give a presentation in class, they thought their world was going to end and that they would faint, or worse, in front of everyone. But they fought back, and they kept going. Every day. That's bravery, and that is to be respected and congratulated.

These books were written to help young people get the facts about mental illness. Facts go a long way to dispel stigma. Knowing the facts gives students the opportunity to help others to know and understand. If your student lives with someone with mental illness, these books can help students know a bit more about what to expect. If they are concerned about someone, or even about themselves, these books are meant to provide some answers and a place to start.

The topics covered in this series are those that seem most relevant for middle schoolers—disorders that they are most likely to come into contact with or to be curious about. Schizophrenia is a rare illness, but it is an illness with many misconceptions and inaccurate portrayals in media. Anxiety and depressive disorders, on the other hand, are quite common. Most of our youth have likely had personal experience of anxiety or depression, or knowledge of someone who struggles with these symptoms.

As a teacher or a librarian, thank you for taking part in dispelling myths and bringing facts to your children and students. Thank you for caring about the brave soldiers who live and work with mental illness. These reference books are for all of them, and also for those of us who have the good fortune to work with and know them.

—Anne S. Walters, PhD
Chief Psychologist, Emma Pendleton Bradley Hospital
Clinical Professor, Alpert Medical School/Brown University

CHAPTER ONE

WHAT IS A DRUG?

Words to Understand

addiction: a strong physical and/or mental need for a particular substance or activity.

asphyxiation: when oxygen is cut off.

depressant: a substance that slows down bodily functions.

hypnotic: a type of drug that causes sleep.

moderation: limited in amount, not extreme.

psychoactive: something that has an effect on the mind and behavior.

sedative: a substance that makes a person calm or sleepy.

seizures: sudden, involuntary physical reactions, sometimes caused by a chemical imbalance in the body.

stimulant: a substance that speeds up bodily functions.

If you have a health problem, a doctor might suggest you take pills that can make you feel better. You've probably heard an adult say that she's useless before she's had her morning coffee. And many adults would also say that a barbecue just isn't a barbecue without hamburgers, hot dogs, . . . and a cold beer.

These things—alcohol, medicine, and the caffeine in coffee—have something in common. They are all types of drugs. Drugs affect our brains, bodies, and behavior when we eat, drink, smoke, breathe, or inject them.

If you have asthma, you probably keep an inhaler handy, with medicine to help you breathe better.

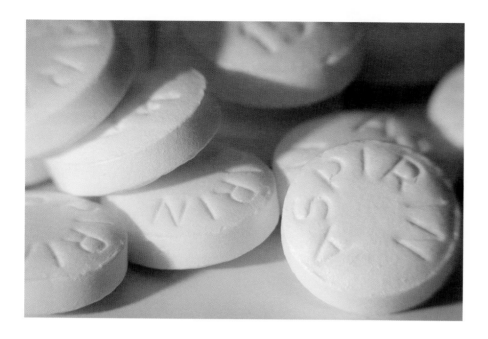

Aspirin is a very common over-the-counter drug. It has been around since the late 1800s. The main ingredient in aspirin, found in willow bark, has been used as a pain reliever for far longer than that.

Not all drugs are bad. Medicine that's prescribed by a doctor can make you healthier or even save your life. Some drugs are harmless in small quantities. But when used too much—or when used by the wrong person—any drug can have negative consequences.

Types of Drugs

Different types of drugs have different effects on the human body. Some, like caffeine, have such minor effects that we barely think of them as drugs at all. Others are so deadly that the government has made them illegal. This chapter will talk about some types of drugs and what they do. Because drugs are such a huge topic, this book will focus on the ones you are most likely to encounter in daily life.

Medicine. There are a huge number of medicines that people can take for different physical and mental problems. Some are called *over-the-counter* drugs because any adult can buy them in a store. For example, if you have a headache, you might take an

Don't share prescriptions with friends. Drugs can affect people in different ways; what is good for you could be a big danger to someone else.

over-the-counter drug like aspirin. Others are called *prescription drugs* because you can only get them with permission from a doctor. For example, if you have very bad headaches, a doctor might give you a prescription drug like Imitrex.

In reality, it is all too common for people to buy or steal other people's prescription drugs. One often-abused class of drugs is *opioids*. These are **depressants** that are used for their pain-killing effects. Morphine, codeine, and oxycodone are all opioids. Doctors prescribe them to people with serious pain. But they are frequently abused by people who don't have real medical needs. (Heroin is also an opioid, but it is illegal and has no medical use.)

Like opioids, drugs called **sedatives** and **hypnotics** have important uses in medicine. They can be very helpful to people with real psychological problems. But, also like opioids, they are often abused by people who do not really need them. Sometimes even people who need them can begin to take too much, which can lead to problems with **addiction**.

It is a very bad idea to take someone else's medicine. For one thing, if the prescription was written for someone bigger than you, the drug could be too strong. It could make you sick, put you in a coma, or kill you. There is also the very serious possibility of addiction, which we will discuss in the next chapter.

Caffeine. This substance is found in coffee, tea, chocolate, and most sodas. "Energy drinks" also have a lot of caffeine. It is considered to be a minor **stimulant**—its effects are not that strong or long-lasting. However, taking in large amounts of caffeine over a short time—or doing it many times over a

For most people, there is no harm in having a cup of coffee with friends. But caffeine is still a drug, and you should be aware of how it affects you.

longer period—can make people sick. It can also interfere with appetite and sleep.

Alcohol. Wine, beer, and cocktails all contain ethyl alcohol, which is a depressant. Although people may seem more "up" after drinking alcohol, inside their bodies, things are slowing down. When used by adults in **moderation**, and—this is very important—when *not driving*, alcohol is not highly dangerous. But if too much alcohol is consumed too quickly—which is called "binge drinking"—alcohol poisoning can result. **Seizures**, choking, and **asphyxiation** are just a few of the possible effects. Meanwhile, if used in large quantities over a long period of time, alcohol can contribute to organ damage, heart disease, and some types of cancer. In fact, alcohol abuse is the third most common cause of preventable death in the United States.

The effects of ethyl alcohol on the body are not the only issue. Just as important are its effects on the mind. Alcohol interferes with our ability to make good decisions. This can

SNIFFING

There are lots of ways that drugs can be taken into the body. People drink coffee and alcohol, and they smoke cigarettes and pot. But there's another way people, especially kids, take drugs into the body: inhaling.

It may seem weird that simply sniffing something could qualify as "doing drugs." But the chemicals in glue, gasoline, and other substances travel through the nose and eventually reach the brain. Some of these chemicals are extremely powerful. In fact, inhalants are also among the most dangerous drugs. Some can kill instantly, while others can cause permanent brain damage.

A DEADLY COMBINATION

A popular trend among younger people is to switch between alcoholic drinks and energy drinks, or even to combine the two into one. Many brands of malt liquor, for example, have a high caffeine content, and this is usually not reported on the label.

Caffeine counteracts the depressant effect of the alcohol. On its own, alcohol will eventually make you sleepy. But when caffeine is added, that is less likely to happen. People like this because they can "party" longer without getting tired.

This is a very dangerous game. Combining the two drugs means that people don't realize just how much alcohol they have consumed. This makes both alcohol poisoning and alcohol-related injuries much more likely.

lead to many risky behaviors, such as drunk driving, that can end in injury or death. According to the Centers for Disease Control and Prevention (CDC), alcohol is responsible for about 88,000 deaths per year—that includes more than 4,000 deaths of people under age 21.

Cannabis. This is the drug in marijuana (also called "pot," "grass," or "weed"). Like alcohol, it is considered to be a depressant. The **psychoactive** ingredient in cannabis is a chemical called THC (tetrahydrocannabinol). Marijuana is often smoked—in cigarette form or in pipes—but it can be taken as a pill or even mixed into food.

DID YOU KNOW?

It is a myth that marijuana is not addictive. People who start smoking marijuana at a young age have about a 1 in 6 chance of becoming addicted.

Some people use marijuana for medical reasons. It has been found to be helpful to people with cancer, multiple sclerosis, an eye condition called glaucoma, and conditions causing long-term pain. Other people use marijuana because it can bring a feeling of relaxation.

However, marijuana can have a bad effect on the lungs and heart, especially when used over long periods. Doctors especially worry about marijuana use in young people,

Antismoking campaigns are not new. This poster was part of a 1950s antismoking campaign, probably in Nigeria.

whose brains are still developing. They fear that long-term marijuana use can result in permanent problems with thinking and memory. One New Zealand study found that teens who smoked marijuana heavily went on to lose an average of eight IQ points in adulthood.

Nicotine. This is the addictive ingredient in cigarettes, which are made from tobacco plants. However, although cigarettes begin as plants, cigarette companies add many other chemicals to them. You have probably heard about the many health problems caused by cigarettes. They include various cancers and very serious heart problems. Chewing tobacco also has serious health risks.

Unfortunately, nicotine is also one of the most addictive of all drugs. And unlike caffeine, there is no "good" or "safe" amount of cigarettes. The only safe approach to smoking is to never start.

Text-Dependent Questions

1. What are some different types of drugs?
2. What are the problems associated with taking someone else's prescription drugs?
3. What are the possible effects of alcohol on the body and mind?

Research Project

Learn about the history of cigarettes in our country: when they were first used, when doctors realized they were so harmful, and when laws about smoking in public places were first introduced. Write a short summary of the change in our acceptance of smoking.

CHAPTER TWO

DRUGS AND ALCOHOL IN SOCIETY

Words to Understand

abstain: to choose not to take part in a particular activity.

fermentation: a chemical process that, for example, turns grapes into wine.

We don't know the exact moment when the very first drug was used. It's possible that it happened by accident. When early humans were searching for plants to eat, they may have discovered a substance with the power to alter the brain. Once the discovery was made, it's likely that some people continued using the substance to achieve the same effect.

A Brief History of Drugs and Alcohol

Beverages (such as wine and beer) have been a part of the human experience for as long as there have been humans. For example, archaeologists have found jugs that probably held an early form of beer in the Neolithic period (about

The heads of poppies, which have been used to make opium for thousands of years.

10,000 BCE). Drinks made through **fermentation** soon became a key part of many religious rituals. We also know that people living on the island of Cyprus dissolved opium in both wine and water. Cyprus also exported opium to Egypt as early as 1500 BCE. This means that drugs have not only been *used* for a very long time—they have also been part of the economy for nearly as long.

Where there is trade, there is also conflict. Substance-related abuse helped cause the Opium War between China and Great Britain (1839–1842). Great Britain had brought opium into China, where it was traded for other goods. The result was widespread addiction among the Chinese people. During the war, China unsuccessfully tried to stop the importation of opium into the country.

Meanwhile, ingredients were extracted from opium and prescribed by physicians in the treatment of a wide variety of illnesses. Substances like morphine and cocaine were legal and readily available. Many soldiers returned home from the US Civil War addicted to morphine, which had been given to them for pain caused by wounds on the battlefield. Ironically, when heroin was first produced, in 1874, it was thought that this drug would provide a cure for morphine addiction.

As substance-related disorders became prevalent and some individuals died because of them, people began to recognize the dangers of addiction. In the latter part of the 19th century and the early 20th century, countries began to pass laws to control mind-altering substances.

DID YOU KNOW?

According to the Bible, the first vineyard was planted by Noah. Historians think the vineyard in question was on Mount Ararat, which is in modern Turkey.

This is why, even today, you must be a particular age to drink alcohol or to buy cigarettes. Drugs and alcohol can have extreme effects on bodies that are still developing. Laws try to prevent young people from taking drugs that could hurt their development.

Drugs and Alcohol Today

Because there are so many possible bad effects of drugs, you might think life would be easier if we just never took them at all. And as we mentioned in the previous chapter, when it comes to cigarettes or illegal street drugs, that's definitely true.

Hospital stewards in front of their tents in Petersburg, Virginia, in 1864. Civil War doctors treated patients with many addictive drugs that are illegal today.

In fact, there are a lot of people who feel that their lives are much better when they **abstain** from drugs and alcohol completely. For example, Muslim people do not drink alcohol, while people who practice the Mormon faith avoid not only alcohol but also caffeine. People who are Christian Scientists tend to avoid taking medication in most cases. Plenty of other people decide to abstain for personal reasons that have nothing to do with religion: they might not care for the taste of alcohol, for example; or they might have had a family member who struggled with addiction.

But other people feel that there are lots of instances where drugs are not harmful and are even beneficial. For example, people who deal with chronic pain need to take drugs regularly in order to just live their lives. Meanwhile, doctors have found that in small quantities, drinking wine or coffee can actually provide health benefits. Studies have suggested that moderate amounts of wine can be good for the human

Grape vines in a Sonoma, California, vineyard. Grapes contain a substance called resveratrol, which might have some health benefits.

ALCOHOL USE BY SELECTED COUNTRY, 2004

Country	Liters (per person/year)
Iran	0.00
Somalia	0.00
Bangladesh	0.00
Indonesia	0.10
Egypt	0.10
Morocco	0.41
Senegal	0.48
Benin	1.22
Turkey	1.48
Guatemala	1.64
Israel	1.99
Nicaragua	2.53
Zambia	3.02
Trinidad and Tobago	3.22
Jamaica	3.37
Philippines	3.75
China	4.45
Brazil	5.32
Norway	5.81
Colombia	5.92
Haiti	6.51
Rwanda	6.80
Sweden	6.86

Country	Liters (per person/year)
Japan	7.38
South Korea	7.81
Belarus	8.12
Canada	8.26
Thailand	8.47
United States	8.51
Argentina	8.55
Poland	8.68
Venezuela	8.78
Italy	9.14
Australia	9.19
Bahamas	9.21
Greece	9.30
New Zealand	9.79
United Kingdom	10.39
Russia	10.58
Denmark	11.93
Spain	12.25
Germany	12.89
Bermuda	12.92
France	13.54
Ireland	14.45
Luxembourg	17.54

In 2004, the World Health Organization (WHO) published a report about alcohol usage around the world. Countries listed with zero alcohol consumption have majority Muslim populations; Muslim law (Sharia) forbids the drinking of alcohol. (It's possible that some people disobey that law, but this was not noted by the WHO.)

heart, while caffeine consumption may have an association with lower rates of dementia and certain cancers.

So the question is, if we choose to include these substances in our lives, how do we embrace the good impacts while limiting the bad ones? There are a few things we can do:

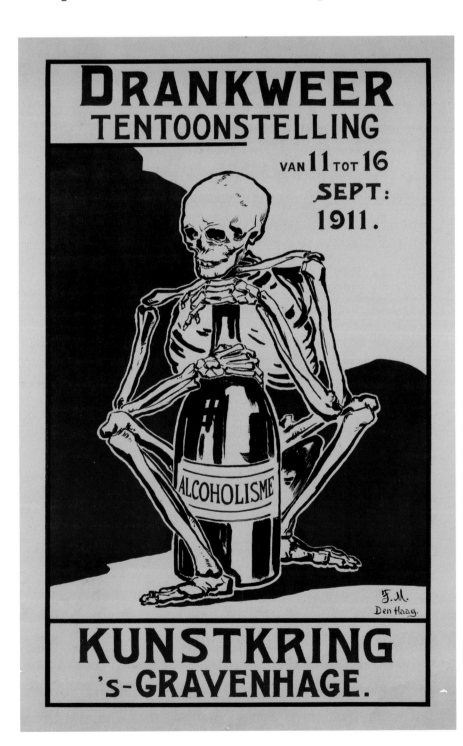

Doctors have been aware of the potential negative effects of alcohol for a very long time. This poster is from an exhibition on alcohol abuse held in the Netherlands in 1911.

- **Practice moderation.** Legal drugs like caffeine and alcohol can usually be used in small amounts without doing any real harm. But bingeing is not good for any part of the body.

- **Avoid other people's drugs.** Every bottle of prescription drugs has a name printed on the label. If that name isn't yours, put it down.

- **Understand that laws have reasons.** Certain drugs are illegal because they can easily destroy your life. Alcohol, on the other hand, is legal for adults but not for kids, because it isn't safe for younger people. It's important to remember that these rules are not designed to keep something "fun" away from you. These laws exist to help keep you safe.

But even when we try to practice moderation and follow the rules, the truth is that some people—both adults and kids—can develop problems with drugs and alcohol. The next chapters will discuss what those problems look like and how people can get help.

Text-Dependent Questions

1. How do we think drugs were discovered by early humans?
2. What are some historical examples of humans using drugs or alcohol?
3. Name some types of people who abstain from drugs and alcohol.

Research Project

Find out more about the rules different religions have relating to drugs and alcohol. Why did those rules develop? Prepare a table with your findings, listing the different religions and their rules and reasons.

CHAPTER THREE

WHAT IS DEPENDENCE?

Words to Understand

dependent: needing something a lot.

induced: brought on.

intoxication: an excited state in which a person is not in control of his actions.

perception: awareness or understanding of something.

recreational: done for fun, or with no specific reason.

withdrawal: taking something away.

As human beings, we depend on eating, drinking, and breathing to stay alive. Some people also depend on particular medicines to stay healthy. For example, people with diabetes need to carefully monitor a bodily substance called insulin. If their insulin levels get too low, they must inject some more so that they don't get sick.

A lot of adults feel like they "depend" on their morning coffee. They have trouble waking up in the morning if they don't get that jolt of caffeine. While it is not great to be **dependent** on caffeine, doctors don't usually worry about it too much. (There are a small number people with severe caffeine addictions, and they may need the help of a doctor to stop.)

Most people can usually break the coffee habit without too much trouble. Avoiding caffeine will probably cause the person to have some headaches at first—the pain is caused by the

People who are used to consuming a lot of caffeine will probably feel a bit ill on the first day they quit. Fortunately, the withdrawal symptoms usually do not last very long.

body craving the caffeine but not getting it. Doctors call this a **withdrawal** symptom. But in a few days or so, the body will adjust to living without caffeine, and the headaches will go away.

Other forms of dependence are more troubling. For example, you may have heard someone talk about how hard it is to quit smoking. There are two main reasons for this: mental and physical. First, smoking becomes a habit that people simply get used to doing—this is the mental part of the dependency. And second, the body gets used to having nicotine on a regular basis. When the nicotine is taken away, the withdrawal symptoms can be rough. People can feel grouchy and even ill. Doctors all agree that it is well worth suffering through the withdrawal in order to quit smoking. But ask anyone who has quit—it's very difficult to do!

Substance-Related Disorders

It can be hard for other people to understand why a person would keep smoking even when he knows it's bad for him. But this is how an **addiction** works. People who are addicted to something keep on using or doing that thing, even when they know they shouldn't. As strange as it sounds, they often feel like they *have to* continue even when they don't *want to* do it anymore.

If a person becomes so dependent on a drug that he keeps taking it even though it hurts him, we describe that condition as a substance-use disorder. A substance-use disorder involves serious and negative consequences from regular use of a substance over a 12-month period. When a person has this disorder, he continues to use the substance even though many problems occur as a result.

Opposite page: The media often make alcohol use look fun, but they don't show all the negative results that can follow.

For example, a teenager who is dependent on alcohol might throw up, have terrible headaches, and generally feel sick from drinking the night before. She might skip class because she feels sick (hungover), or she might do so to spend more time drinking. She might steal money to buy alcohol. She might go to parties with people she doesn't know well—people who could hurt her. She might drive while drunk or get in a car with someone else who's drunk. These are all negative consequences—but someone with a substance-use disorder will continue using the drug anyway.

A second type of drug and alcohol problem is called substance-**induced** disorder. This term refers to problems beyond the actual addiction. Substance-induced disorders include the physical or mental problems that can be caused by usage of the drug—such the withdrawal symptoms discussed above. Sometimes these two types of disorder—substance-use and substance-induced—are simply collected together and called substance-related disorders.

Symptoms of Substance-Related Disorders

Symptoms of drug and alcohol disorders vary a lot, depending on the substance being used. They are also determined by the person's body chemistry, the amount of substance used, the duration of use, and other factors. The most common symptoms include poor thinking, judgment, **perception**, and attention. The person may have difficulty staying awake, or he might have so much energy that he is awake and active all night.

The way someone acts toward others will often be far different than it would be if the substance were not being used. When used **recreationally** (as opposed to use for

SUBSTANCE-RELATED DISORDERS: DIAGNOSTIC CRITERIA

The *Diagnostic and Statistical Manual of Mental Disorders* (*DSM*) lists 11 criteria that doctors use to diagnose a substance-related disorder. The criteria are divided into four groups.

Impaired Control

These criteria relate to the difficulty someone has in stopping use of the drug.

1. The person takes larger amounts than intended, or takes the substance for a longer period than intended.
2. The person attempts to "cut back" but can't.
3. The person devotes large amounts of time to getting, using, and recovering from the drug.
4. The person feels regular cravings for the drug.

Social Impairment

These criteria relate to the negative impact of the drug on the person's life.

5. Drug use interferes with duties at work or school.
6. Drug use causes problems with friends, family members, or coworkers.
7. The person gives up other activities in favor of using the drug.

Risky Use

These criteria relate to the person's use of the drug even when it is likely to cause harm.

8. The person uses the drug in situations that are physically dangerous.
9. The person continues using the drug even though he or she knows that it causes physical or emotional problems.

Pharmacological Criteria

These relate to the chemical impact of the drug on the body.

10. The person has an increased tolerance for the drug, meaning that it takes more to achieve the same effect.
11. The person experiences withdrawal symptoms when the drug is not used.

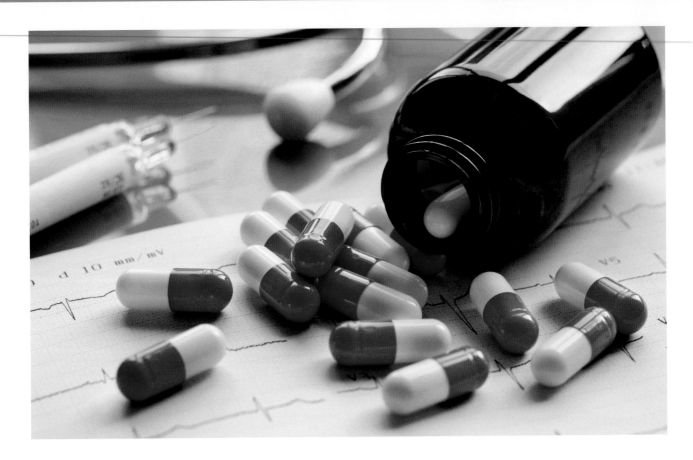

According to the National Institute on Drug Abuse, although the US population is only 5 percent of the world, Americans consume 75 percent of all prescription drugs.

medical reasons), drugs create a state of **intoxication**. As a result, people say and do things while using drugs and alcohol that they would not normally say or do. It's common for people with this disorder to feel shame as a result of things they did or said while intoxicated. It's also common for people to not even *remember* the things they said or did while intoxicated—this is called a "blackout" and is usually a sign of a serious problem.

Why Is Dependence a Problem?

Remember that when you use a drug, you interfere with the brain's natural chemical activities. If the drug is used regularly, the brain gets used to the addictive substances and begins to "expect" them. This is why, as discussed in chapter one, someone who normally drinks coffee every day might get a headache if she tries to skip a day. Over time, tolerance builds up, and our coffee drinker might need two cups of coffee to feel the effect she used to get from one.

It's important to understand that all drugs—even medicine given by doctors—can be dangerous if used incorrectly. Depending on the drug, vital organs like the liver and kidneys can be injured. In some cases, such as with alcohol or cigarettes, the likelihood of developing cancer or heart disease will increase.

As tolerance builds, it takes more of the drug for the person to feel the effects. The amount of the drug used then increases. And, in turn, so do the negative impacts on the body. Meanwhile, the negative impacts on the person's life will also increase. But if he tries to stop using the drug, he may find he is unable to do so. In fact, it can be dangerous for

ADDICTION OR DISORDER?

Doctors receive special training to help people with substance-related disorders.

You've probably heard about "drug addiction," or maybe you've heard a particular person described as a "drug addict." But most doctors prefer to avoid using the word *addiction*. Although it is very commonly used in regular speech (and is used in this book), as a diagnosis, the word addiction is too vague. *Substance-related disorder* is the preferred term because it is more specific and less negative sounding.

WHAT IS TOLERANCE?

Most people who abuse a drug will develop "tolerance" to the chemical effects on the body. This means that they have to take more to get the effect they want.

Some people brag that they can "hold their liquor"; in other words, they are proud of their ability to drink so much without acting drunk. They don't realize, though, that this is actually a symptom of alcohol abuse.

someone with a severe drug dependence to stop all at once. Quitting after the brain has built up tolerance to a substance causes even more chemical disruption in the brain. This is why people with substance-induced disorders usually need some form of medical help to quit.

Text-Dependent Questions

1. What is withdrawal?
2. What is tolerance, and why is it a problem?
3. What are some signs of a possible substance-use disorder?

Research Project

Do some research on the negative effects of alcohol use on health. Cover topics such as: how much do doctors think is okay, what health problems can result from excess drinking, and how can an adult tell what is too much drinking and what is a moderate amount. Write a short paragraph on each of these topics.

CHAPTER FOUR

TREATING DRUG AND ALCOHOL DEPENDENCE

Words to Understand

acupuncture: an ancient Chinese treatment that involves pricking the body with needles at specific points.

cognitive: having to do with the thought process.

relapse: getting worse after a period of getting better; for example, when someone who had stopped using drugs starts using again.

stigma: negative ideas or feelings about something.

It is not easy, but with effort, people can recover from substance-related disorders. Unfortunately, withdrawal symptoms are often extremely unpleasant. Until fairly recently, people with substance-related disorders were expected to conquer them "cold turkey." This expression means stopping the use of a substance on your own, and then suffering through whatever happens next.

Fortunately, treatment facilities now exist where people with substance-related disorders can get professional help for their problems. The most successful treatments often combine the use of medication with therapy.

DID YOU KNOW?

Relapses are very common when someone attempts to recover from a substance-related disorder. It does not mean that the recovery is a failure. It just means the person has more work to do to get better.

Medication

Over the years, scientists have worked to develop medications that can help to reduce the symptoms of withdrawal. Medications have also been developed to help individuals avoid **relapse**.

It's important to understand that substance-related disorders are complex. People who have these disorders are suffering from mental, emotional, and physical problems. So while medicine can be helpful in treatment, it is usually not enough to break the pattern of substance addiction. People have a better chance at recovery if medications are combined with counseling or participation in a recovery program.

Therapy

Everything we see and do, even talking, has the power to affect our brains. Talking to a therapist or members of a self-help group can be a very powerful form of treatment for a substance-related disorders.

Cognitive-behavioral therapy (CBT), a type of therapy involving training in social and coping skills, is among the most successful. The goal is for the person to be better able to express herself and to interact appropriately in various situations. These skills can reduce a person's daily anxieties and struggles and may make it easier for her to avoid the temptation to use drugs. CBT also involves looking at the thoughts or "triggers" that cause drug use, and teaching ways to change or avoid these triggers. Sometimes CBT is used with a technique called *motivational interviewing*. This helps people to identify the pros and cons of changing their behavior in order to help them make needed changes.

Family therapy is also useful in dealing with substance-related disorders. It helps a family know how to help the individual in crisis and how to keep the family unit healthy and together.

People working to overcome a substance-related disorder sometimes struggle with how to spend time with their friends, because many social gatherings involve alcohol. But it is possible to have fun without drinking.

Other Treatments

Many people with anxiety or depression find relief through meditation and relaxation techniques. These same techniques have also helped people with substance problems.

Breathing deeply helps to clear your mind of all thoughts and to calm and relax your body. With meditation, a person allows thoughts to float through his mind, while he remains detached. Gentle stretching, deep breathing, and mind-soothing exercises like those found in yoga can be very helpful in reducing the depression that often comes with having a substance-related disorder.

Some people report that **acupuncture** has helped to reduce their cravings for specific substances. It has been used successfully to treat cravings in individuals addicted to cocaine and nicotine.

Alternative remedies for substance abuse disorders may also include herbs, vitamins, and dietary supplements, some of which

Some people find meditation very helpful in battling addiction.

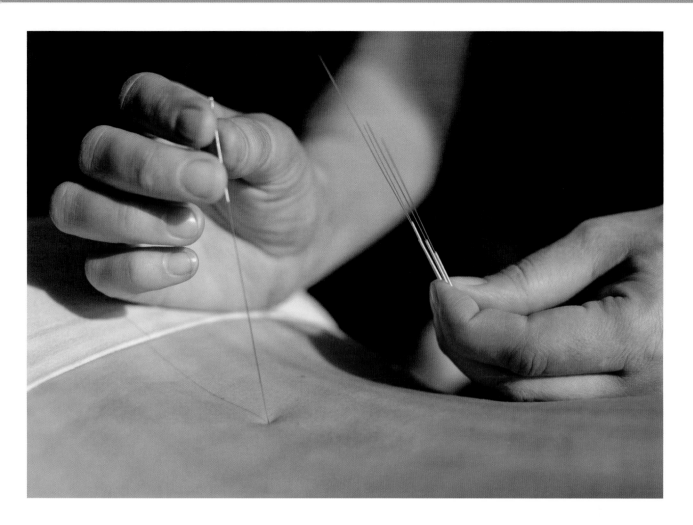

have been used for centuries by peoples around the world. But you should use caution when taking these substances. Herbs, vitamins, and dietary supplements are not regulated by the government in the way that traditional medicines are.

Acupuncture is another alternative therapy that some people with substance-related disorders find helpful.

The 12 Steps

The best-known treatment for substance abuse in North America is Alcoholics Anonymous (AA). AA does not advocate the use of any psychiatric medications as part of treatment. Instead, it relies on attending regular group meetings and following a 12-step program. The 12 steps were written by the earliest members of AA to describe their process of recovery. For example, the first step is for the person to admit that he

Talking to others who are struggling with similar challenges can be very helpful.

or she is "powerless over alcohol." Later steps require the person to make lists of people they hurt in the past and to seek forgiveness. AA is a self-directed program—meaning people follow the steps at their own pace. Members of the group reach out to one another, to help them by sharing their own experiences.

AA has changed the lives of many people, but it is not the answer for everyone. Some people, for example, have a hard time with the religious component of AA. A number of the 12 steps relate to the addicted person's relationship with God, and people who are not religious may find those steps uncomfortable or inappropriate. It's important to know that AA does not insist that all members believe in a Christian God. Meanwhile, there are increasing numbers of "humanist" or "agnostic" AA meetings, which follow the same basic rules but do not put as much emphasis on the religious aspect.

Many other 12-step programs have been modeled after AA, including Narcotics Anonymous, Cocaine Anonymous, and so on. Two important ones to know about are Al-Anon and Alateen; these groups are for the families of people with alcohol dependency.

If Someone You Know Has a Disorder

If you know someone with a substance-related disorder, try to have compassion. This is a very painful type of disorder to have, and the social **stigma** can be very difficult to deal with.

That said, it can be hard to cope with a family member or close friend who has a substance-related disorder. Here are a few things you can do:

- **Admit the problem.** Your family member may not want to admit that she has a problem. But you can still admit it—to yourself, to a counselor, or to a friend. It's the first step toward making things better.
- **Get help.** If your family member will accept help, that's great—but if not, you can still get help on your own. For example, the groups Alateen, Narcotics Anonymous, and Alcoholics Anonymous all have resources for family members. It's *especially* important to get help if you don't feel safe in your house. If that's the case, you might call the National Domestic Violence Hotline at (800) 799-SAFE.
- **Remember, it's not your fault.** People do not drink too much or use drugs because of what someone else does. Even if your family member tries to blame you for his

problem, it's not true. Always remember that the family member has a disease, and you did not give it to him.

If you think you may be at risk for developing a substance-related disorder, discuss your concerns with your parents, a trusted teacher, your doctor, or a counselor. If you are already using one of the substances that can cause a disorder, try to stop. If you can't, the disorder already exists, and you need to seek advice right away. Many communities have centers that offer resources to help with drug or alcohol use, or hotlines that you can call anonymously.

Help is available to assist you with this problem. It's not easy, but don't give up. Recovering from a substance-related disorder can be done—and it can save your life.

It's very tough to have a family member with a substance-related disorder. Be sure to take care of yourself and seek out other people who can support you.

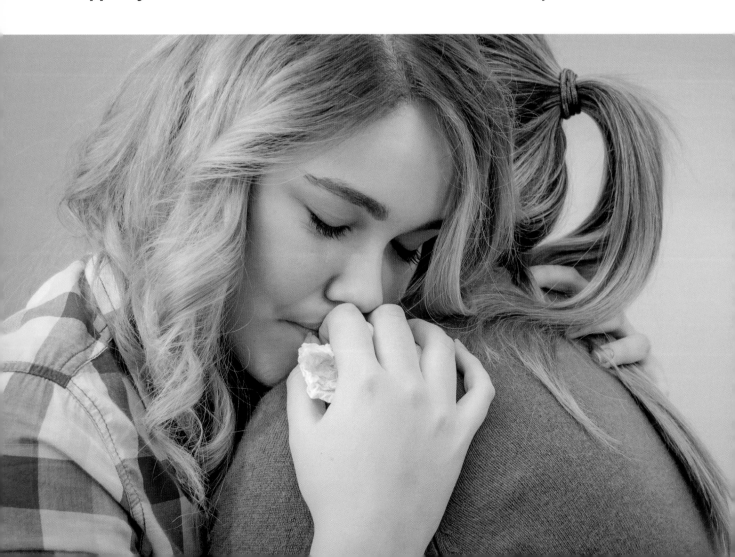

Text-Dependent Questions

1. What is the most effective treatment plan for someone with a substance-related disorder?
2. Why is therapy effective?
3. What are the main aspects of AA?

Research Project

Find out more about what resources are available in your area. Does your school have a D.A.R.E. (Drug Abuse Resistance Education) program, for example? If so, what services does it offer? You might search online for 2-1-1, a program run by the United Way, which collects information about local resources for dealing with substance-related disorders (including smoking). Also check to see what groups (AA, Alateen, and so on) meet in your area. Write a short paper that lists the different services available.

Further Reading

BOOKS

Babbit, Nikki. *Adolescent Drug & Alcohol Abuse: How to Spot It, Stop It, and Get Help for Your Family*. Sebastopol, CA: O'Reilly & Associates, 2000.

Davenport-Hines, Richard. *The Pursuit of Oblivion: A Global History of Narcotics*. New York: W. W. Norton, 2004.

Volpicelli, Joseph, and Maia Szalavitz. *Recovery Options: The Complete Guide*. New York: John Wiley & Sons, 2000.

Wetherall, Charles F. *Quit: Read This Book and Stop Smoking*. Philadelphia, PA: Running Press, 2001.

ONLINE

Addictions.org. "Recovery Stories." www.addictions.org/stories.htm.

Alcoholics Anonymous. www.aa.org.

National Institute on Drug Abuse. www.drugabuse.gov.

Substance Abuse and Mental Health Services Administration. www.samhsa.gov.

LOSING HOPE?

This free, confidential phone number will connect you to counselors who can help.

National Suicide Prevention Lifeline

1-800-273-TALK (1-800-273-8255)

Series Glossary

acute: happening powerfully for a short period of time.

affect: as a noun, the way someone seems on the outside—including attitude, emotion, and voice (pronounced with the emphasis on the first syllable, "AFF-eckt").

atypical: different from what is usually expected.

bipolar: involving two, opposite ends.

chronic: happening again and again over a long period of time.

comorbidity: two or more illnesses appearing at the same time.

correlation: a relationship or connection.

delusion: a false belief with no connection to reality.

dementia: a mental disorder, featuring severe memory loss.

denial: refusal to admit that there is a problem.

depressant: a substance that slows down bodily functions.

depression: a feeling of hopelessness and lack of energy.

deprivation: a hurtful lack of something important.

diagnose: to identify a problem.

empathy: understanding someone else's situation and feelings.

epidemic: a widespread illness.

euphoria: a feeling of extreme, even overwhelming, happiness.

hallucination: something a person sees or hears that is not really there.

heredity: the passing of a trait from parents to children.

hormone: a substance in the body that helps it function properly.

hypnotic: a type of drug that causes sleep.

impulsivity: the tendency to act without thinking.

inattention: distraction; not paying attention.

insomnia: inability to fall asleep and/or stay asleep.

licensed: having an official document proving one is capable with a certain set of skills.

manic: a high level of excitement or energy.

misdiagnose: to incorrectly identify a problem.

moderation: limited in amount, not extreme.

noncompliance: refusing to follow rules or do as instructed.

onset: the beginning of something; pronounced like "on" and "set."

outpatient: medical care that happens while a patient continues to live at home.

overdiagnose: to determine more people have a certain illness than actually do.

pediatricians: doctors who treat children and young adults.

perception: awareness or understanding of reality.

practitioner: a person who actively participates in a particular field.

predisposition: to be more likely to do something, either due to your personality or biology.

psychiatric: having to do with mental illness.

psychiatrist: a medical doctor who specializes in mental disorders.

psychoactive: something that has an effect on the mind and behavior.

psychosis: a severe mental disorder where the person loses touch with reality.

psychosocial: the interaction between someone's thoughts and the outside world of relationships.

psychotherapy: treatment for mental disorders.

relapse: getting worse after a period of getting better.

spectrum: a range; in medicine, from less extreme to more extreme.

stereotype: a simplified idea about a type of person, not connected to actual individuals.

stimulant: a substance that speeds up bodily functions.

therapy: treatment of a problem; can be done with medicine or simply by talking with a therapist.

trigger: something that causes something else.

Index

Page numbers in *italics* refer to photographs.

About the Author

H. W. POOLE is a writer and editor of books for young people, such as the *Horrors of History* series (Charlesbridge). She is also responsible for many critically acclaimed reference books, including *Political Handbook of the World* (CQ Press) and the *Encyclopedia of Terrorism* (SAGE). She was coauthor and editor of the *History of the Internet* (ABC-CLIO), which won the 2000 American Library Association RUSA award.

About the Advisor

ANNE S. WALTERS is Clinical Associate Professor of Psychiatry and Human Behavior. She is the Clinical Director of the Children's Partial Hospital Program at Bradley Hospital, a program that provides partial hospital level of care for children ages 7–12 and their families. She also serves as Chief Psychologist for Bradley Hospital. She is actively involved in teaching activities within the Clinical Psychology Training Programs of the Alpert Medical School of Brown University and serves as Child Track Seminar Co-Coordinator. Dr. Walters completed her undergraduate work at Duke University, graduate school at Georgia State University, internship at UTexas Health Science Center, and postdoctoral fellowship at Brown University. Her interests lie in the area of program development, treatment of severe psychiatric disorders in children, and psychotic spectrum disorders.

Photo Credits

Photos are for illustrative purposes only; individuals depicted in the photos, both on the cover and throughout this book, are only models.

Cover Photo: Dollar Photo Club/flass100

Dollar Photo Club: 10 highwaystarz; 11 blueskies9; 13 Igor Mojzes; 15 Monkey Business; 22 Gyula Gyukli; 27 Subbotina Anna; 32 Brian Jackson; 33 Monkey Business; 34 Africa Studio; 37 Monkey Business; 38 carla9; 39 yunava1; 40 Monkey Business; 42 doble.d. **iStock.com:** 12 Fotosmurf03; 19 HynekKalista; 29 b-d-s. **Library of Congress:** 21. **Wellcome Library, London:** 16, 24.